Life of Fred®

Farming

Life of Fred®
Farming

Stanley F. Schmidt, Ph.D.

Polka Dot Publishing

ISBN: 978-0-9791072-9-0

Library of Congress Catalog Number: 2011908674
Printed and bound in the United States of America

Polka Dot Publishing   Reno, Nevada

To order copies of books in the Life of Fred series,

visit our website PolkaDotPublishing.com

Questions or comments? Email the author at lifeoffred@yahoo.com

Fourth printing

Life of Fred: Farming was illustrated by the author with additional clip art furnished under license
from Nova Development Corporation, which holds the copyright to that art.

for Goodness' sake

or as J.S. Bach—who was
never noted for his plain
English—often expressed it:

Ad Majorem Dei Gloriam
(to the greater glory of God)

If you happen to spot an error that the author, the publisher, and the printer missed, please let us know with an e-mail to: lifeoffred@yahoo.com

As a reward, we'll e-mail back to you a list of all the corrections that readers have reported.

A Note Before We Begin
the Sixth Book in the Series

The year was 1970. I bought a small fish tank and put it on my desk. I filled it with water and added a plastic plant and a thermometer.

An instant later, my one-year-old had converted it into part of her education.

Jill had climbed up on her own. The thermometer was in her left hand. The water and the plastic plant were about to be investigated.

I guess you could call it part of home schooling.

Kids love to learn. They want to know everything about everything:

Education

◊ Why are some curbs painted red?
◊ What do pennies taste like?
◊ Where do babies come from?
◊ If f:A→B and g:B→A are two one-to-one functions, how can we show that there must exist a function h:A→B that is both one-to-one and onto?*

It takes a lot of effort to kill a child's love of learning. If you are interested in doing that, here's how to do it:

How to Kill the Love of Learning

1. Lock a child in a room ("classroom") for hours with 20 other kids.
2. Insert a guard ("teacher") who really doesn't love learning. (It helps if the teacher majored in "education" or in "general studies," rather than in a real academic major.) People who teach history should love history.

_____

* I get this question all the time. We answer it in the first chapter of *Life of Fred: Calculus.*

Those who teach math should love mathematics. The Acid Test: Do the teachers who teach XYZ talk about XYZ with their spouses and friends? Do they read and learn new things about XYZ?

Would you want to study oenology (pronounced ee-KNOLL-eh-gee) from someone who doesn't drink?

3. Make sure there are lots of external rewards (A+!) and punishments attached to the "education." Don't let the learning itself be the reward. Focus on getting the diploma or the degree.

4. Do not let a child get carried away with any subject. Set a schedule of 50 minutes per day for each of the five required subjects. If a child gets fascinated with how log cabins are built or with reading Dante's description of the horrors of hell, make sure they do it "on their own time." This will teach them that "education" and their own interests are two different things.

5. Finally, if you want to kill a child's love of learning, it is critically important that you do not become a good role model. Don't do any serious, sustained, and joyful adult learning of your own. Just read murder mysteries or romance novels, talk on the phone a lot, and watch daytime television.

❁   ❁   ❁

On the positive side . . . that one-year-old who had climbed up to study my aquarium never spent a day in an American high school classroom. Home schooling doesn't take as long as government schooling. There are no football rallies or teacher-training days to get in the way of learning.

> At 13½ she finished her high school studies and became a college student.
> At 15 she headed to Europe for a year as an exchange student.
> At 20 she graduated from the University of California, Berkeley.

Isn't it amazing what a little work with a fish tank will do?

❁   ❁   ❁

BY NOW YOU KNOW
HOW THESE BOOKS ARE ORGANIZED

Each chapter has six pages. At the end of each chapter is a Your Turn to Play. Your child writes out all the answers to each Your Turn to Play before looking at the answers on the next page.

Just reading the questions and looking at the answers is passive learning. It doesn't work. It's like trying to learn how to ride a bicycle by just reading about it.

CALCULATORS?

Not now.

Kill the Love of Learning
and you get . . .

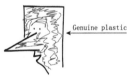

Genuine plastic

Contents

Chapter One
Working at Night

Kingie is just your average doll who enjoys doing oil painting. When Fred was about four days old, he got Kingie as a free toy at King of French Fries.

It wasn't until Fred (and Kingie) became five years old that Fred learned how good Kingie was at art.

Most of the time Kingie did his oil painting when Fred was gone. When Fred was teaching or visiting Edgewood, Kentucky, Kingie would take out his oil paints and begin working.

Kingie did his best when it was quiet and he could concentrate on the work he was doing. No radio. No television.

During the night when Fred was sleeping was a perfect time for Kingie to paint. When Fred was awake, he liked to talk to Kingie and hug him. That made it difficult for Kingie to pay attention to his painting.

Dolls (and people) often do trashy work when there are too many distractions.

small essay

A Secret about Dolls

Have you ever noticed that many dolls have this big vacant stare? Their big glassy eyes don't seem to be looking at anything.

asleep

If you ask them what is 8 + 9, they will just look at you and not say 17.

Everyone knows that eight plus nine is seventeen, but many dolls will just sit there. Do you know why?

The answer is that many dolls stay up all night. While you are sleeping, they use that quiet time to get their work done.

By morning, when you wake up, they are really tired. Some dolls sleep all day with their eyes open.

Now you know their secret.

Fred was sleeping. He was tired out from his trip to Edgewood. It was a quarter to one in the morning.

Kingie was just finishing up his second oil painting of the

12:45 a.m.

Woman Descending Stairs
by Kingie

night. He had used a dry brush to make the picture grainy. That gave a dreamlike feeling to the painting.

As with many of Kingie's paintings, you are drawn into the painting.

You start to think:

◇ Those stairs seem steep.

◇ Where is she going?

◇ Why is she holding her back?

With great art, you remember it long after you have seen it.

But dolls are not the only nocturnal[*] things. As Kingie worked, he could hear some sounds coming from Fred's backpack. It was a cute little mouse that had sneaked into his backpack when he was on the bus to Edgewood.

The mouse came up and stood beside Kingie. He gave the mouse a little pat on the head. Here was an animal that Kingie liked. He was terrified of cats and dogs, but mice were different. Kingie now had a pet of his own.

---

[*] KNOCK-turn-el Active at night.

Kingie knew that mice eat just about anything. They are not obligate carnivores (like cats) who must eat meat.

Kingie tiptoed over to Fred's desk. He didn't want to wake Fred who was in his sleeping bag under the desk.

Everyone knows that Fred is not a big eater.* Whenever he gets any food, he sticks it in his pocket and says, "for later." Then he puts it in his desk. When Kingie opened the desk, he found 14 pounds of food.

There was 5 lbs. in one drawer and 9 lbs. in another drawer. (lbs. is an abbreviation for pounds.)

There were 6 lbs. of sandwiches and 8 lbs. of other stuff.

$$
\begin{array}{r} 5 \\ + \ 9 \\ \hline 14 \end{array}
\qquad
\begin{array}{r} 6 \\ + \ 8 \\ \hline 14 \end{array}
$$

Please memorize these before you turn the page. There is no hurry. The mouse is enjoying one of Fred's sandwiches.

---

* *Fred is not a big eater* is an example of litotes. (LIE-toe-tease) Here are other examples of litotes: *A billion dollars ($1,000,000,000) is not a small amount of money. The Pacific Ocean is not a little pond. A toothpick is not a fat log. A dime is not a heavy coin.*

Litotes are fun to invent.

Please take out a piece of paper and write down the answers. Then turn the page and compare your answers to mine.

You will learn a lot more that way than just reading the questions and reading the answers.

Your Turn to Play

1. Name a value for x that will make this true:
x + 6 = 14.

2. Name a value for y to make this true: $14 - y = 5$.

3. Name a value for z that will make this true: z > 99.

4. A die has six different faces: ⚀⚁⚂⚃⚄⚅.
If you shook two dice, how could they add up to 10?

5. (Harder question) We know that there were 5 lbs. of food in one drawer and 9 lbs. in another drawer.

We also know that of the 14 lbs. of food, 6 lbs. are sandwiches.

Does that mean that both drawers must contain sandwiches?

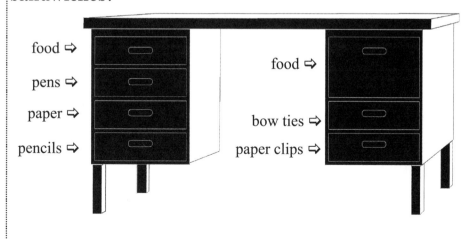

food ⇨

pens ⇨

paper ⇨

pencils ⇨

food ⇨

bow ties ⇨

paper clips ⇨

.... ANSWERS ....

1. If x is 8, then x + 6 = 14 is true.

2. If y is 9, then 14 − y = 5 is true.

3. z > 99 means "z is greater than 99."

There are many possible answers you might name.

If z is 100, then z > 99 is true.

If z = 103, then z > 99 is true.

If z = 1,000,000, then z > 99 is true.

If z were equal to a googol, then z > 99 would be true.

A googol is 1 followed by a hundred zeros.

This is a googol:
10,000,000,000,000,000,000,000,000,000,000,000,
000,000,000,000,000,000,000,000,000,000,000,000,
000,000,000,000,000,000,000,000.

4. To have two dice add up to 10, you could have:

✓ the first die be ⚃ and the second die be ⚅ or

✓ the first die be ⚄ and the second die be ⚄ or

✓ the first die be ⚅ and the second die be ⚃.

5. Both drawers do not have to contain sandwiches. (They could, but they don't have to.) All six pounds of sandwiches could be in the bigger drawer that contains nine pounds of food.

Chapter Two
Good and Great

12:55 a.m.

Kingie went back to his oil painting. It was five minutes to one in the morning. He had five or six hours left before dawn.

He had the three things necessary in order to become a great artist: ① He loved his work; ② He had natural talent; ③ He practiced many hours each day.

Do you want to become a great piano player? Love it, Have talent, and Work hard.

Do you want to become a great teacher? Love it, Have talent, and Work hard.

Do you want to become a great paleobotanist?* Love it, Have talent, and Work hard.

---

*A paleobotanist is someone who studies fossil plants.
My favorite specialty is paleobiogeography. Paleobiogeographers study the distribution of ancient plants and animals on the earth. If I count correctly, *paleobiogeographer* has nine syllables.

Most people are not "great." Being great is for one person in a million.

On the other hand, being good at something is what each of us can do.

Do you want to be a good baseball player? A good mathematician? A good parent? A good pizza chef? That's much easier.

Pick any two: Love it, Have talent, and Work hard.

Kingie's pet mouse liked Fred's office. There was plenty of food, and there were lots of fun places to explore. She ran around on Fred's bookshelves. She went in Kingie's fort.

When Fred had a cat, Kingie built his fort in the corner of the office. It was a place he could go to protect himself. He didn't want to become a cat toy. It was Kingie's private place that no big person could ever go inside.

Most people don't consider Fred a big person. He is only three feet tall, the same as a yardstick.

But from Kingie's point of view, Fred is big.

Kingie is only six inches tall.
If you put two of Kingie's brothers
on top of each other, they would
be 12 inches tall.

    6"   (" means inches)
+ 6"
‾‾‾‾‾
 12"

Twelve inches equal one foot. 12" = 1'

Three feet equal one yard. 1' + 1' + 1' = 1 yard.

It was dark inside Kingie's fort until the
mouse turned on the lights. On one wall in the
living room Kingie had put up pictures of his
five brothers who also lived in Kansas.

Kenneth   Kendric   Karney   Kermit   Kory

Kingie put those pictures up on the wall
because he loved his brothers and he didn't want
to forget what they looked like.

On another wall in the living room, Kingie had put up pictures of his brothers who lived in Georgia: Gael, Gallagher, Galvin, Garrett, and Gilroy.*

In one corner of the room was a grand piano. Kingie had it specially built to fit him. It was a small grand piano.** Often when Fred was away Kingie would come into his fort and play his piano to relax.

When the mouse ran down the keys, it sounded like this:

Mouse on Keyboard

which could also be written:

------

* We leave it to you to imagine what the pictures of those five brothers in Georgia looked like.

** Grand pianos are huge. You can't have a small grand piano. If you were a lot older, we could mention that *small grand piano* is an **oxymoron**. (ox-ee-MORE-on) A quiet rock concert is an oxymoron. A hungry Fred. A two-ton mosquito. A trouble-free life.

Kingie shut the front door to his fort so the piano playing wouldn't wake Fred.

Quietly take out a pencil and a piece of paper, because it is . . .

Your Turn to Play

1. Copy these on your paper and answer them:

$$
\begin{array}{ccc}
5 & 8 & 46 \\
+\ 7 & +\ 9 & +\ 36 \\
\hline
\end{array}
$$

2. Name a value for x that will make $8 + 4 = x$ true.

3. Here are 100 boxes. There are 10 stacks and each stack has 10 boxes in it.
What percent of the boxes are black?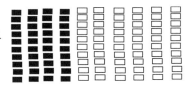

4. Here is another stack of 100 boxes. What percent of them are gray?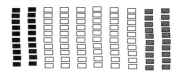

5. Counting by twos, write all the numbers from 44 to 60.

· · · · · · ·ANSWERS · · · · · · ·

1.

	5	8	$\overset{1}{4}6$
	+ 7	+ 9	+ 36
	12	17	82

To add these two-digit numbers together, you start on the right.

6 + 6 equals 12. Write down the 2 and carry the one.

2. If x is equal to 12, then 8 + 4 = x is true.

3. Of the 100 boxes, 40 of them are black. 40% of the boxes are black.

4. Of the 100 boxes, 20 of them are gray. 20% of the boxes are gray.

5. 44, 46, 48, 50, 52, 54, 56, 58, 60.

Chapter Three
Exploring the Fort

The mouse was having fun exploring Kingie's fort. She hopped off of the piano and ran up the stairs. At the top of the stairs was a large archway.

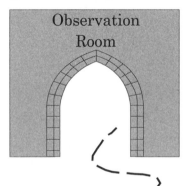

Observation Room

The mouse couldn't read. She just ran inside.

When Kingie had built his fort, he wanted to be able to look out and see whether there was a cat in Fred's office. The second story of his fort was his observation room. It has lots of big windows.

From the observation room, the mouse could see Kingie painting. She could see Fred sleeping under the desk. She could see all of Fred's books that covered the walls of his office.

She wondered why Fred liked to read. She and her brothers and sisters and her parents never learned to read. They just watched television and ate snacks.

Time Out!

Not all the mysteries of life can be explained. But there is one mystery that we will now explain.

This mystery has never before been revealed in any other arithmetic book that has ever been written.

When your parents buy a box of mouse poison at the hardware store, it is labeled in big letters: MOUSE POISON. DANGER! DO NOT EAT!

This is a mystery. The box should read: Delicious Mouse Food. Very Tasty! Eat Lots of It.

The secret is . . .

mice can't read.

The mouse ran up another flight of stairs to the top floor. This room was very dark. It had no windows. ☞ zero windows

This is the room where Kingie kept some of the money he received from selling his oil paintings. When the mouse turned on the light, she saw 16 safes that were full of money. There were 9 on the left wall and 7 on the right wall.

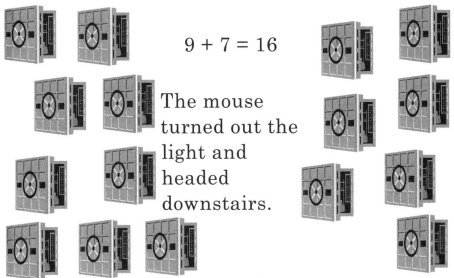

$$9 + 7 = 16$$

The mouse turned out the light and headed downstairs.

Some notes about what we have just seen:

♪#1: Mice are not very interested in money. No mother mouse ever told her kids, "I want you to grow up and become a millionaire."

♪#2: Kingie has made a lot of money as an artist. No other artist in the whole world needs 16 safes to hold the sales from art. Most artists do not make a lot of money.

Most baseball players do not make a lot of money.
Most boxers do not make a lot of money.
Most musicians do not make a lot of money.
You do art,
    or play baseball,
        or box,
           or play music
    because you like doing those things—not to get rich.

♪#3: If you spend your whole life making money, you will only miss out on one thing: Life.*

♪#4: There is something **very special** about
$$9 + 7 = 16.$$

It is the very last addition fact that you have to learn.

In *Life of Fred: Apples*, we did all the numbers that add to 7. (We started out slowly because you were very young back then.)

In *Life of Fred: Butterflies*, we did all the numbers that add to 9—such as 4 + 5, 3 + 6, and 2 + 7.

In *Life of Fred: Cats*, we did the numbers that add to 11 and add to 13.

In *Life of Fred: Dogs*, we did all the doubles—2 + 2, 3 + 3, 4 + 4, etc. and we did the numbers that add to 15 and add to 17.

In *Life of Fred: Edgewood*, we did the numbers that add to 8, 10, and 12.

———————————————

* Or as Ralph Waldo Emerson wrote, "Money often costs too much."

And now in this book, we did the numbers that add to 14 and 16.

You are done with addition.

You will never have to count on your fingers again.

All that remains is some practice to increase your speed and accuracy.[*]

Your Turn to Play

1. Complete this sentence: The commutative law of addition says that 9 + 7 will give the same answer as
_____.

2. Find the value of x that makes this true: 5 + x = 14.

3. One yard is equal to how many feet?

4. How many rows does this matrix have? (From *Life of Fred: Edgewood*)

$$\begin{pmatrix} 5 & 8 & 9 & 2 \\ 6 & 7 & 1 & 0 \\ 4 & 4 & 3 & 9 \end{pmatrix}$$

5. What is the median average of 700, 85, 16, 82, 3?

---

[*] I, your author, am 69 years old. Each month when I get the bank statement for my checking account, I balance it with pencil and paper to retain my addition and subtraction skills. Over the years, practice has made addition easier and easier.

......ANSWERS.......

1. The commutative law of addition says that 9 + 7 will give the same answer as 7 + 9.

2. If x is equal to 9, then 5 + x = 14 will be true.

3. One yard is equal to 3 feet.

4. It has 3 rows. (It also has 4 columns.)

5. The first step in finding the median average is to arrange the numbers from smallest to largest:

3, 16, 82, 85, 700. The second step is to pick the number in the middle. The median average is 82.

Now that you have all the addition facts from 1 + 1 up to 9 + 9, the key to mastery will be to use those facts.

A Row of Practice.

Cover the gray answers with a blank sheet of paper. Write your answers on your paper. Then after you have done the whole row, check your answers. *If your answers are not all correct, then get out a new sheet of paper and do this row again.*

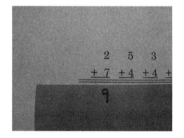

$$
\begin{array}{ccccc}
63 & 9 & 55 & 4 & 73 \\
+\ 75 & -\ 6 & +\ 88 & +\ 9 & +\ 96 \\
\hline
138 & 3 & 143 & 13 & 169
\end{array}
$$

Chapter Four
The Least and the Most

The mouse was having fun exploring all the rooms in Kingie's fort. As she was coming down the stairs from the room with the 16 (9 + 7 = 16) safes in it, she met Kingie going up those stairs. He had just sold another three paintings and was carrying a big bag of cash to put in one of the safes.

Normally, it takes several weeks before an oil painting will dry and can be sold. Until then, it can easily be smeared.

The demand for Kingie's art work is so great that people will call Kingie on his cell phone and ask if his newest work is done yet. They will buy it before it has dried.

Tall House
by Kingie

Kingie was doing what he loved to do, which is paint. The money or the fame was not important to him.

The mouse continued exploring Kingie's fort. She came down to the living room where the small grand piano and the pictures of Kingie's brothers were. There were two doors—a red door and a blue door—that led to rooms she hadn't seen yet.

She squeezed underneath the red door and entered the biggest,

      largest,

           most enormous,

              hugest room

                    she

                    had

                    ever

                    seen.

And it was empty.

Giant white walls with no pictures on them. No furniture. Not even dust on the floor. And it was very quiet.

She squeezed back under the red door and went back into the living room. She climbed on the piano and ran over part of the keyboard (from left to right):

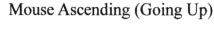

She hoped that the room behind the blue door would be more interesting.

She squeezed under the blue door and found a room filled with . . . everything!

What a mess! she thought. *This needs to get cleaned up and organized.*

Like any good mouse, she started by gathering together four pieces of cheese.

This is the **set** of those four pieces of cheese: { , , , }.

A set is the same thing as a group or a collection. We have lots of different words for *set*.

A flock of birds = a set of birds.

A collection of marbles = a set of marbles.

A herd of cows = a set of cows.

A group of people = a set of people.

A colony of ants = a set of ants.

A congregation of people in church = a set of people in church.

A pride of lions = a set of lions.

Flock, collection, herd, group, colony . . . are called **collective nouns.** English is often harder than math. You have to memorize which collective noun goes with which set. You have to say "school of fish" and not "herd of fish."

In mathematics, we just use the word *set.* And a set can contain any bunch of things. It doesn't have to be all cheeses: { ⬠, ◐, ⬭, ⬚ }.

In this room that contained everything, the mouse could have assembled this set: {✂, ✎, ❄, 🍒, ⬚, π}.

The spelling rule for mathematical sets is easy: Please don't list the same member of the set twice. Don't write {π, ⬚, π, ☎}.

The reason for this rule is that it makes it easier to count the number of members of a set. You might accidentally say that the cardinality of {π, ⬚, π, ☎} is 4, when it is actually only 3.

In English, the spelling rules are harder than calculus. Why don't they spell it *kayyoss* instead of *chaos*?

Combining Things

In English . . .   one mouse, two mice

one cat, two cats,

one sheep, two sheep.

With numbers . . . $2 + 2 = 4$

$3 + 3 = 6$

$9 + 7 = 16.$

With sets . . . $\{A, ☎\} \cup \{◨, ✈\} = \{A, ☎, ◨, ✈\}$

$\{★, 🍒, \pi\} \cup \{■, ♥\} = \{★, 🍒, \pi, ■, ♥\}$

$\{C, D\} \cup \{C\} = \{C, D\}.^{*}$

Your Turn to Play

Multiple-choice questions

1. You can't *add* sets together because:

    A) Sets are not numbers

    B) Sets are made of chocolate

2. $\{🍒\} \cup \{✈\}$ is called the **union** of $\{🍒\}$ and $\{✈\}$. The little symbol "$\cup$" reminds you of:

    A) <u>u</u>nion

    B) somebody's nose

    C) the month of February

---

* Not $\{C, D, C\}$ because of the spelling rule for sets.

```
. . . . . . . ANSWERS . . . . . . .
```

1. If you wrote that you can't *add* sets together because sets are made of chocolate, you get a grade of NC. (NC stands for "Not Close.")

Addition is really great for numbers, but you can't use it for sets.

You can't add together a square and a triangle.

You can't add together Kansas and Kentucky.

You can't add together Orion and the Big Dipper.

2. Any of these answers can be correct. If, somehow, the little symbol "∪" reminds you of February, who can say that you are wrong?

∪ might remind some people of a handkerchief.

∪ might remind some people of the book of Micah.

But ∪ was probably chosen because of <u>union</u>.

Addition is a lot harder than taking the union of two sets. Here is <u>A Row of Practice</u>. *If your answers are not all correct, then get out a new sheet of paper and do this row again.*

29	16	45	8	54
+ 75	− 7	+ 38	+ 7	+ 66
104	9	83	15	120

Chapter Five
Mouse Brains

The room behind the blue door was filled with everything that the mouse could have fun with. If she wanted to study chemistry, she could assemble a chemistry lab.

If she wanted to cook, there was everything she needed.

In that room there were books, balloons, bananas, and the supergiant star Betelgeuse.

The mouse tried to imagine the set of all things that begin with the letter B: {books, balloons, bananas, Betelgeuse, bathtubs, bats, Bavaria, Boston, belts, bisons, bones, boomerangs, brains, buildings, Budapest (which is the capital of Hungary), bunnies, butterflies, . . . }.

This was too much for a mouse brain. She headed back into the living room and jumped up and down on one note on the piano in order to clear her brain.

Middle C Played 24 Times

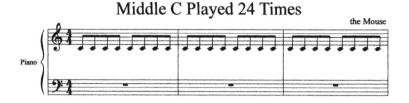

Time Out!

One of the biggest challenges that any good teacher has is: How much of the Big Truth should I tell my students?

The world is much stranger than the stuff you see on television. Much more weird.

Ask a biologist to give you a definition of what things are alive and what are not. They are not sure. They can't agree. (See *Life of Fred: Pre-Algebra 1 with Biology*.)

Ask a physicist, "What makes things fall? What is gravity? Why do all electrons weigh as much as they do?" They really don't know!

There are strange math truths about the room behind the red door (the room that was empty) and about the room behind the blue door (the room that contained everything).

The mouse was overwhelmed just thinking about the set of all things beginning with the letter B. Her mouse brain was overloaded, and she ran and played on the piano to clear her head.

Here are some truths about the room with the red door and the room with the blue door *that most adults don't know*.

The Red Door Room

Most children's math books will point out that in this big empty room you could form the **empty set**: { }. It's the set that has no members. That is not surprising.

What *is* surprising is what you can do in this big empty room.

Of course, you can't do biology. There are no frogs or trees in this room.

Of course, you can't do physics. There are no magnets or wires in this room.

What you can do in this room is ALL of mathematics—just starting with the empty set. That is hard to believe, but it's true.

For example, we start by getting the number 0. Simply ask, "What is the cardinality of { }?"

You want the number 1? That's the cardinality of this set: { {} }. That set has one member in it.

After we have the whole numbers 0, 1, 2, 3, 4, 5, . . . , we can get the negative numbers –1, –2, –3, –4 . . . and all the rest of the numbers.

We can even get lines and squares and triangles without having to draw them.*

If you woke up tomorrow morning and all your rubber duckies, all your waffles— everything!—were gone, then every part of science would be gone . . . except mathematics.

The Blue Door Room

This gets even more weird.

In the old days, we mathematicians used to talk about the Universal set—the set that contained everything. We imagined taking everything and sticking it into one giant set. The Universal set was soooooo big that it even contained the Universal set!

---

* The only high school geometry book that shows you how geometry can be done without any diagrams at all is *Life of Fred: Geometry*. (It's in the last chapter.)

Then about a hundred years ago, a mathematician proved that the Universal set can't exist. There can't be a room behind the blue door that contains everything!*

So the red door room (the empty one) contains all of math and the blue door room (that contains everything) doesn't exist.

World's Shortest Your Turn to Play

1. {a, b, c} ∪ {c, d, e}

---

* Do not read this footnote until you are old enough to have finished calculus. Math majors in their junior year of college are usually the only ones who are shown this proof that the Universal set can't exist.

      Step one: Define a normal set as any set that does not contain itself as a member. (Sometimes a normal set is called a Russell set.) The Universal set (call it U) is not a normal set since it is a member of itself. U ∈ U. "∈" means *is a member of.*

      The set of all sets mentioned in this book (call it M) is not a normal set. I mentioned M in this book, so M ∈ M.

      Step two: Consider the set of all normal sets. (Call it N.) If U exists, then N must exist because is a subset of U. The existence of the universal set U is what is going to get us into trouble.

      Step three: Now we ask the question, "Is N a member of N?" N ∈ N?
If you say yes, that means N ∈ N. Then N is normal because it belongs to the set of all normal sets. Then N couldn't be a member of itself by the definition of normal. But we just said N ∈ N.
If you say no, that means N is not a member of itself. Then N must be normal by the definition of normal. But if N is normal, it is a member of the set of all normal sets, which is written as N ∈ N. But we just said that N is not a member of itself.

      In step two, we said that if U exists, then N must exist. In step three, we showed that N existing results in nonsense. Therefore, U cannot exist.

┌───┐

    ....**ANSWERS**........

1. {a, b, c} ∪ {c, d, e} = {a ,b, c, d, e}

└───┘

English majors sometimes tend to be very wordy. One of them might look at the answer to the Your Turn to Play and say, "It appears to me that the sum of the cardinalities of two sets may not equal the cardinality of their union."

$$\{a, b, c\} \cup \{c, d, e\} = \{a, b, c, d, e\}$$

$$3 \quad + \quad 3 \quad \neq \quad 5$$

Instead of using too many words (being prolix), mathematicians sometimes use few words (that's called being laconic):

For any two sets, A and B, $\text{card}A + \text{card}B \geq \text{card}(A \cup B)$.

A Row of Practice. *If your answers are not all correct, then get out a new sheet of paper and do this row again.*

75	17	45	9	59
+ 77	− 9	+ 84	+ 6	+ 69
152	8	129	15	128

Chapter Six
Saturday Morning

Fred had been happily sleeping. It felt good to be tucked away in his three-foot sleeping bag. It was a chance to rest after a long week.

It was the seventh day of the week. There are no classes at KITTENS on Saturday, so he knew he would not be teaching today. He was hoping that the university president would get back from skiing and allow classes to resume on Monday.

2:40 a.m.

It was twenty minutes to three in the morning, and Fred was dreaming. He dreamed about his kitty. He dreamed about the thirty dogs he had owned. He dreamed about Max and his family in Missouri. They were all good dreams.

He even dreamed about how he had once put his ear muffs on his nose to keep his nose warm.

All happy dreams.

What Fred didn't realize was that the warm furry feeling of having ear muffs on your nose wasn't what was really happening.

Fred didn't know that he had accidentally brought home the mouse from the Edgewood trip. He didn't know that the mouse had been running all around his office and had explored all the rooms in Kingie's fort.

And Fred didn't know that the mouse was now standing on his nose.

Fred is terrified of mice.

Had Fred opened his eyes, he would have been staring right into the face of the mouse.

Not a good way to wake up

Instead, he slept.

Fred has had many good things happen in his life. This was one of them. If he had woken up at 2:40 in the morning, that would have been a very bad start for his day. Instead, he had a beautiful dream about having a "nose muff" to keep his nose warm. We often have blessings in life that we are not aware of.

The mouse jumped off Fred's nose and headed back to nibble more of Fred's sandwiches. Then she squeezed under the office door and headed down the hallway toward the nine vending machines.

In an office down the hall from Fred's is a man that teaches about the music of ancient Greece. He is not a very nice man. (You'll learn more about him in *Life of Fred: Pre-Algebra 2 with Economics*.) He owns an obligate carnivore, which he lets run loose in the hallways of the Math building.

End of mouse.

❀   ❀   ❀

Fred slept until five minutes to seven. By the time he woke up, his doll had put away all the oil painting work that he had done during the night. Kingie just stood there with a big vacant stare. Fred didn't know that Kingie had made $4,800 (four thousand, eight hundred dollars) during the night from the sale of his paintings.

6:55 a.m.

Fred gave Kingie a hug and noticed that his doll smelled a little like oil paint. Then he walked down the hallway to the restroom to wash his face. Fred was eager to begin a happy Saturday.

On the way back to his office, he passed a cat, which had a big smile on its face. It looked like it was also having a happy Saturday.

Fred picked up the newspaper.

THE KITTEN Caboodle

The Official Campus Newspaper of KITTENS University   Saturday 6:50 a.m.   10¢

FLASH!

University President Breaks Leg in Skiing Accident

KANSAS: Yes, he broke it. The president said, "I will not be able to perform the duties of university president for a couple of months." He reported that he will be heading to Hawaii while his leg heals.

President says he thinks it is his right leg that is broken.

The vice president is unavailable. He is vacationing in France.

The assistant vice president is on a beef-inspection trip to Argentina.

The sub-assistant vice president can't be located.

The next in line for leadership of the university is Samuel P. Wistrom, the janitor for the second and third floors of the math building. (continued on page two)

—page two—

Sam the Jan., as everyone at KITTENS calls him, has made the following statement: "Now that I'm acting president, call me Sir Wistrom."

Someone pointed out that having "Sir" in front of your name means that you are a knight.

Editorial

The president has a broken leg. He says he can't "perform the duties of university president."

The only thing he has ever done recently is cancel classes. You can do that with a broken leg.

Your Turn to Play

1. Kingie made $4,800 selling three of his paintings. If each of those paintings was $1,600, would that equal $4,800?

2. The mouse was on Fred's nose at 2:40 a.m., and Fred awoke at 6:55 a.m. How long was it from 2:40 to 6:55?

(Hints: First figure out how long it was from 2:40 to 6:40. Then figure out how long it was from 6:40 to 6:55.)

3. {cat} ∪ {rat, cat, mat}

4. Is ∪ commutative?

........ANSWERS........

1. The question asks whether 1600 + 1600 + 1600 will equal 4800.

$$
\begin{array}{r}
\overset{\scriptstyle 1}{1600} \\
1600 \\
+\ 1600 \\
\hline
4800
\end{array}
$$

The answer is yes.

> You start on the right.
> The zeros add up easily.
> Next you have to add up the three 6s. 6 + 6 = 12, and 12 plus another 6 is 18. You write down the 8 and carry the one.
> The four 1s add to 4.

2. From 2:40 to 6:40 is **4 hours.**

From 6:40 to 6:55 is **15 minutes.**

The total time from 2:40 to 6:55 is 4 hours and 15 minutes.

3. {cat} ∪ {rat, cat, mat} = {rat, cat, mat}.

Or {cat, rat, mat} or {mat, cat, rat}. The order you list the members of a set does not matter.

4. ➤Is the union of sets commutative?

➤If I take the union of the set of stuff in my left pocket with the set of stuff in my right pocket, will I get the same answer if I take the union of the stuff in my right pocket with the set of stuff in my left pocket?

➤Does {a, b} ∪ {c} give me the same answer as {c} ∪ {a, b}?

The answer is yes to all of these questions.

Chapter Seven
Off to the Farm

Fred read the advertisement about Fun Farming! That looked exciting. He had never had the chance to pet a chicken.

He borrowed $300 from Kingie and promised to pay him back when he received his salary from KITTENS at the beginning of March.

The address given in the ad was 123 Snakefoot Road. Fred found Snakefoot Road on a map. It was five miles south of the university.

Perfect! thought Fred. *I can jog and be there when the farm opens.*

Fred changed into his jogging clothes and headed out the door, down the hallway, past the nine vending machines (four on one side and five on the other), down the two flights of stairs, out into the sunshine, and then started jogging south.

Kingie got out his oil paints. He mumbled to himself, "It shouldn't cost $100 to visit a farm. Farms don't *open* in the morning. And you don't pet chickens—they aren't dogs."

Meanwhile, Fred couldn't be happier. He sang, ♪"I'm off to see the Fun Farm." ♫

The sun warmed up his left cheek. When you are heading south, the morning sun (in the east) is on your left.

To understand this diagram,
you may need to turn this book
upside down.

Now as you are heading
south, the sun is hitting
your left cheek.

Heading south

As he jogged, he did the math in his head. He had $300 and it cost $100 to get in the Fun Farm:

$$\begin{array}{r} \$300 \\ - \ \underline{\$100} \end{array}$$

That left $200 to spend on "meals and other stuff."

He imagined cows saying, "Moo." Sheep saying, "Baa." Roosters saying, "Cock-a-doodle doo.*"

Fred jogged past a giant green head. He heard it say:

Only three miles to the Fun Farm!

---

* In German, you don't say cock-a-doodle-doo. You say kikeriki.
In French, it's cocorico. In Italian, chicchirichì.

Does that mean that you can tell what country you are in by listening to roosters?

    5   miles from KITTENS to the farm

– 3   only three miles left to the farm

    2   Fred had already jogged two miles.

He knew exactly what he would find because he had seen some of Kingie's artwork.

Farmland
by Kingie

Long green rows of crops with mountains in the background.* He knew he would find cows all lined up neatly.

Electric Cows
by Kingie

He didn't know how the farmers got their cows to all stand in a nice line. It was one of the things he wanted to find out at the Fun Farm.

---

* Kansas isn't really noted for its mountains.

Points all in a straight line are
called **collinear** (co-LYNN-ee-err).

Fred giggled and thought,
*would cows in a straight line be
called cow-linear?*

Fred ran past a
large windmill. He
noticed that it was
different than Kingie's
painting of "Farmland."
There were no mountains
in the background.

He ran past some cows.
They weren't "cow-linear"
like Kingie's painting
"Electric Cows."

They were just scattered around in the field
enjoying their breakfast.

When Kingie was doing his paintings in
Fred's office, he was painting pictures of
farmland and of cows *as he imagined them*.

He could put a big mountain in the
background.

He could line up all the cows in a row.

What artists offer is *their view* of the world.

If they wish to paint a freeway, it doesn't have to look like any freeway you have ever seen. They are showing what a freeway looks like to them.

People buy Kingie's art because they like how he sees the world.

This is not Kingie's art. It was drawn by someone who was just learning how to drive.

Your Turn to Play

1. If it is 5 miles from KITTENS to the farm and there was only 1 mile left to get to the farm, how far would Fred have already jogged?

2. Name a value for x that will make this true:

x + 1 = 5.

3. Counting by fives, write the numbers from 100 to 130.

4. If there are 100 cows in the field and 10 of them are brown, what percent (%) of them are brown?

5. If there are 100 cows in the field and 10 of them are brown, how many are not brown?

```
........ANSWERS .......
```

1.   5   miles from KITTENS to the farm
   <u>− 1</u>   only one mile left to the farm
     4   Fred had already jogged four miles.
2. If x is equal to 4, then x + 1 = 5 is true.
3. 100, 105, 110, 115, 120, 125, 130
4. If 10 out of a 100 cows are brown, then 10% of them are brown.
5.   100   cows in field
   <u>− 10</u>   brown cows
      90   that are not brown.   90% are not brown.

A Row of Practice. *If your answers are not all correct, then get out a new sheet of paper and do this row again.*

24	18	54	7	78
+ 68	− 7	+ 89	+ 6	+ 68
92	11	143	13	146

Chapter Eight
Main Entrance

F red was so excited. He pictured himself standing out in the field with his hoe. He was ready to help with the farming.

The advertisement in the newspaper said that he would "Learn to farm," and that he would get to "Pet the animals."

The ad said that it would cost *only* $100/day. Fred wondered what the regular cost for visiting a farm was. *Probably much more,* Fred thought.

Fred didn't know that on many farms in Kansas, if you ask politely, the farm owner will let you work on his farm all day for free.

Fred arrived at the front gate.

The sign was so large. Fred was impressed. Fred knew *This must be a really big and beautiful farm. I hope I will be able to see it all today.* Fred took out $100 so that he could pay quickly. He didn't want to miss a single moment of farm life.

He entered the building under the sign and paid the entrance fee. There was also an amusement tax, a sales tax, and a farm land tax. Fred started with $300. He now had $152.

He came into a large room filled with tables and chairs. He thought this was a classroom where they would teach him everything about farming before he actually got out there in the sun to "work the soil."

He sat down. He wished that he had brought paper and pencil so that he could take notes. A woman came up to him and handed him a menu.

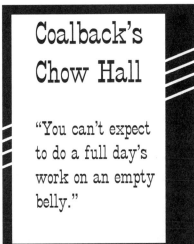

Coalback's
Chow Hall

"You can't expect to do a full day's work on an empty belly."

Fred opened the menu.

The waitress came and asked Fred what he wanted to have. Fred had seen her before, but he couldn't remember where.

Burger	$43
Fries	$18
Cotton Candy	$23
Candy Canes	$11
Sluice	$14
Gum	$ 8

Ask your waitress about the SPECIAL OF THE DAY.

Fred asked, "What is the special of the day?" He hoped that it would be cheaper than the expensive stuff on the menu.

She said, "It's our special Farmer's Nachos—special white sauce and special beans." She turned around and headed away.

Fred realized that she thought he had ordered that.

Time Out!

It is the oldest trick in the book: giving people stuff that they really haven't ordered.

Fred hadn't ordered the Farmer's Nachos.

She knew he hadn't ordered them. When she delivered the nachos to his table, she would lie and say that

he had asked *for* them. In reality,
he had only asked *about* them.

Rather than make a fuss, many
people will just pay for the stuff
they haven't ordered.

If you get stuff that you haven't
ordered, you are not obligated to
pay for it.

Fred wasn't even hungry. In a minute she
came with the Farmer's Nachos on a paper
plate: two nacho chips, some white sauce
(marshmallow sauce!) and three beans (one red,
one green, and one blue). The beans weren't
pinto beans or black beans. They were jelly
beans.

"Eighteen bucks," she demanded. He paid.

He had $152 after paying the entrance fee.

To find out how much he had left subtract
$18 from $152. This is something new.

If the nachos were $21, the subtraction
would be easy.

$$\begin{array}{r} \$152 \\ -\ 21 \\ \hline 131 \end{array}$$

You always start on the right.
$2 - 1 = 1$ and
$5 - 2 = 3$.

But subtracting $18 from $152 is different.

152

− 18   You can't subtract 8 from 2!

You "borrow one" from the 5. $1\overset{4}{\cancel{5}}2$

                                      − 18

And now you can subtract.   134

Your Turn to Play

1. Fred now had $134. He put the Farmer's Nachos in his pocket "for later" since he wasn't hungry. He got some of the marshmallow sauce on his fingers, so he wiped it off with a paper napkin.

The waitress said, "That will be $5 for the paper napkin." Fred paid. How much did he have now?

         134

       − 5

2. The entrance fee was $100. The nachos were $18. The napkin was $5. Find the median average of these three numbers.

3. Fred thought to himself, *These prices are so high. It will cost me a million dollars before I even get to start farming.* Write one million as a numeral.

4. A yard is 36 inches. A meter is about 39 inches. How much longer is a meter than a yard?

```
........ANSWERS .......
```

1.
$$1\overset{2}{\cancel{3}}4$$
$$-\quad 5$$
$$\overline{129}$$

We start on the right.
We can't subtract 5 from 4.
We borrow one from the 3.
5 from 14 is 9.

Fred now has $129.

2. To find the median average of 100, 18, and 5, you first line them up from smallest to largest: 5, 18, 100. Then you pick the number in the middle.

The median average is 18.

3. One million written as a numeral is 1,000,000.

4. A meter is about 3 inches longer than a yard.

$$39$$
$$-36$$
$$\overline{3}$$

A Row of Practice. *Do the whole row before you look at the answers.*

52	45	43	67	197
+ 88	− 7	+ 79	+ 67	+ 368
140	38	122	134	565

Chapter Nine
The Napkin

Fred had a dirty paper napkin in his hands. He read the sign on the wall: "If you leave a dirty napkin on the table—the littering fee is $3."

He saw the trash can. On it was a sign: "Garbage fee is $4."

He thought of offering the napkin to the waitress. Another sign on the wall: "Collection fee of $5 for things handed to the waitress."

He put the napkin in his pocket.

He got up and left the restaurant. He looked on the wall to make sure there wasn't a charge for leaving the chow hall.

He headed toward the door marked EXIT. *Finally,* he thought, *I'll get to do some farming.*

"Hey you. Where are you going with that napkin?"

"Do you mean this one?" Fred asked as he reached into his pocket and took out the napkin. He realized that he had put the napkin in the same pocket as the

Farmer's Nachos and his $129. It was all a sticky mess.

"Were you trying to steal that napkin?"

Steal? Fred thought. *I have never stolen anything in my life. I don't do that.* Fred answered, "No. This napkin is mine. I bought it and paid the waitress $5 for it."

"What do you mean?" the man continued. "You didn't buy that napkin. Five dollars is the rental fee. Do you want me to call the police?"

Fred swallowed. He started sweating. He certainly didn't want to be called a thief. Here is the arithmetic:

$129   Fred started with.

− 29   Money he now handed the man

$100   The money that Fred had in his pocket as he exited the chow hall.

That was an expensive fifty-two dollar breakfast, Fred thought. *I started with $152, and now I have $100. I really want to get out there and do some farming.*

Leaving Coalback's Chow Hall, Fred found himself at

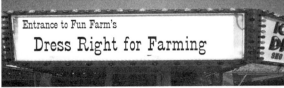

"Hey kid. You can't go farming looking like that." It was Coalback's sister. She worked both as a waitress and as a salesperson in Dress Right for Farming.

Time Out!

You know exactly what was going to happen next. Coalback's sister would tell Fred that he needed a farmer's hat. He needed jeans and a cowboy shirt. He needed farming shoes.

None of the things would fit Fred, and the total cost would be $100.

$$\begin{array}{r} \$100 \\ -\ 100 \\ \hline 0 \end{array}$$

What he would have looked like

But that didn't happen.

The police arrived.

Fred panicked.* *Oh no!* Fred thought. *They have come to arrest me because of something I forgot to pay for.* Fred put his arms up in the air.

The two policemen walked right past Fred. One of them smiled and put Fred's arms down as he passed.

They had come to arrest C. C. Coalback and his sister. The charge was fraud.

Arrest Warrant**

Arrest: *C. C. Coalback and his sister*

Reason: *Fraud* (= lying and trickery to make money)

A) *Selling defective electric heaters.*

B) *Offering "free gym lessons" that really weren't free.*

C) *Overcharging at a farm, a restaurant, and a clothing store.*

---

* The **past tense** of *look* is *looked*. Today I look. Yesterday I looked. The past tense of *talk* is *talked*. *Shout* ≫ *shouted*. *Raise* ≫ *raised*. *Lower* ≫ *lowered*.

But the past tense of *panic* is not *paniced*, but *panicked*.

Today we picnic in the park. Yesterday we picnicked.

** Warrant = authorization. This warrant authorized the police to make an arrest.

The police handcuffed Coalback and his sister, put them in the back of their car, and drove away.

Your Turn to Play

1. {napkin} ∪ {$100, nachos}
2. {napkin, nachos} ∪ {$100, nachos}
3. Sometimes in subtraction you have to "borrow one" more than once.

Let's look at
$$536$$
$$- \ 148$$

You always start on the right.

We can't subtract 8 from 6, so we borrow one.

$$5\overset{2}{\cancel{3}}\cancel{6}$$
$$- 148$$
$$8$$

8 from 16 is 8

But now we can't subtract 4 from 2.

We borrow one from the 5.

$$\overset{4}{\cancel{5}}\ \overset{1\,2}{\cancel{3}}\cancel{6}$$
$$- 148$$
$$388$$

Now it's your turn to play:

$$925$$
$$- 729$$

Good news! You have just done the hard kind of subtraction problems—"borrowing one" more than once.

·······**ANSWERS**·······

1. {napkin} ∪ {$100, nachos} = {napkin, $100, nachos}

2. {napkin, nachos} ∪ {$100, nachos}
    = {napkin, $100, nachos}.

(You do not list the nachos twice.)

3.

$$
\begin{array}{r}
925 \\
-\,729 \\
\end{array}
\quad \rightarrow\rightarrow\rightarrow \quad
\begin{array}{r}
9 \overset{1}{2}{}^{1}5 \\
-\,729 \\
\hline
6 \\
\end{array}
\quad \rightarrow\rightarrow\rightarrow \quad
\begin{array}{r}
\overset{8}{9}\,\overset{1}{2}{}^{1}5 \\
-\,729 \\
\hline
196 \\
\end{array}
$$

Borrow one from the 2

Borrow one from the 9

A Row of Practice. *Do the whole row before you look at the answers.*

98	435	55	74	493
+ 96	− 7	+ 78	+ 67	+ 376
194	428	133	141	869

Chapter Ten
The Farm

The man with the cigar and hat quickly disappeared when the police arrived. That man wasn't Coalback. It certainly wasn't Coalback's sister! It wasn't another employee at the Fun Farm since Coalback made his sister do all the work at the farm.

See you later. I gotta be going.

By not hiring anyone else, he saved a lot of money. And the result was that his sister was completely overworked.

Who was this man? Here is his history.

Before the Fun Farm had opened today, he had sneaked across the back field and into the Coalback Chow Hall without paying the admission fee. He thought that only very rich people would pay $100 to go see a farm. And rich people might be carrying a lot of money with them.

He looked around. Little five-year-old Fred was the only one there. He knew he had to act quickly before Coalback and his sister stole all of Fred's money. He wanted to steal some too.

He pretended he worked at the farm and shouted at Fred, "Hey you. Where are you going with that napkin?"

And he took $29 from Fred.

       ❁   ❁   ❁

Suddenly everything was quiet. Fred was all alone at the farm. He stood there wondering what to do.

He had paid the admission fee, so it wouldn't be stealing to walk around and see the farm. With $100, Farmer's Nachos, and a dirty paper napkin in his pocket, Fred headed outside.

He still wanted to do some work with a hoe. He pictured himself getting rid of the weeds in a vineyard or mixing up some rich brown soil before planting seeds.

Instead, this is what the the Fun Farm looked like: rocks and bricks. It was the worst piece of farmland in Kansas. Coalback had rented it for $10/month from an old man. It used to be an old brick factory that had burned down. The old man had asked Coalback why he wanted to rent this useless property.

Coalback lied, "I'm not sure."

And he never even paid the rent.

Fred didn't know what to do. It was five minutes to nine on a lovely Saturday morning. He was standing in front of acres of bricks.

8:55 a.m.

Fred did what most five-year-olds would do. He decided to go play with the bricks.

He built a little square house out of the bricks. It reminded him of Kingie's fort, but it wasn't as fancy as Kingie's. He called it Fort Fred.

An **acre** is a measure of area.
One square mile is exactly 640 acres.
One acre is 43,560 square feet.
If you draw a square that is about 209 feet on each side, that will be an acre.

Then it fell down. Luckily, Fred wasn't inside.

Fred made ten stacks of bricks. Each stack had ten bricks in it. That represented the $100 that he still had.

Then he stacked up bricks to represent the
$152 he had after he had paid his entrance fee.

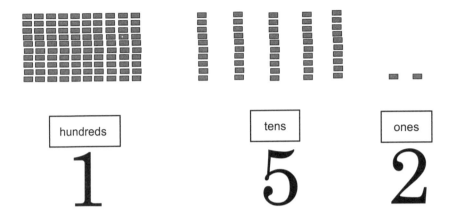

Fred ran out of things to do. There was no
one to play with. There were no animals to pet.

If he had brought a book, he could have sat
on the pile of bricks and read. That would have
been a pleasant way to spend a Saturday
morning. But he didn't have a book.

He tried to make a face out
of bricks, but it didn't look very
good at all. He thought *If Kingie
were here, he could do a much
better job than I.*

Fred headed back through the
chow hall. He turned off the lights and left the
Fun Farm.

As he left, he turned around and looked at the front gate to the farm.

An **n** had fallen off the sign.

Your Turn to Play

1. Are the white dots in **a** collinear?

2. Draw a triangle. Draw a rhombus. Draw a trapezoid.

3. Sometimes, when you want to "borrow one" in a subtraction problem, you can't.

$$
\begin{array}{r}
503 \\
-7 \\
\hline
\end{array}
$$

You can't borrow one from the 0.

Here is the trick: You first borrow one from the 5.

$$
\begin{array}{r}
\overset{4}{5}\,{}^{1}0\;3 \\
-7 \\
\hline
\end{array}
$$

Then borrow one from the 10.

$$
\begin{array}{r}
\overset{4}{5}\,\overset{9}{{}^{1}0}\,{}^{1}3 \\
-7 \\
\hline
496
\end{array}
$$

Your turn:
$$
\begin{array}{r}
405 \\
-8 \\
\hline
\end{array}
$$

········**ANSWERS** ·······

1. Points are collinear if they are all in a straight line. The white dots in  are certainly not collinear.

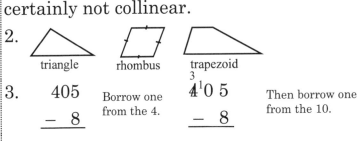

2.

△ triangle   ▱ rhombus   ⬠ trapezoid

3.
$$405$$
$$-\ \ 8$$

Borrow one from the 4.

$$4^{1}0\ 5$$ (with small 3 above)
$$-\ \ 8$$

Then borrow one from the 10.

$$\overset{3}{\cancel{4}}{}^{1}\overset{9}{\cancel{0}}{}^{1}5$$
$$-\ \ \ 8$$
$$\overline{3\ 9\ 7}$$

small essay

What would you do if you owned acres of rocks and bricks? Certainly, you should be able to make more than $10/month.

A) With the bricks you might be able to build a bunch of houses.

B) With a bulldozer, you could smooth all the bricks and rocks and then pave it over and make an airport.

C) Or bulldoze them and build a new brick factory.

A Row of Practice. *Do the whole row before you look at the answers.*

69	826	73	804	229
+ 86	− 8	+ 58	− 67	+ 693
155	818	131	737	922

Chapter Eleven
Not Heading South

The university was five miles north of Fred. It was Saturday, so he didn't have to hurry back to teach classes today.

Fred thought, *What if I headed south and went around the whole world to get back to KITTENS? I bet that would be a long jog.*

The world is about 25,000 miles in circumference. Instead of going 5 miles one way, he could go 24,995 miles the other way.

$$2\overset{4}{\cancel{5}}\overset{9}{\cancel{0}}\overset{9}{\cancel{0}}0$$
$$-\qquad\qquad 5$$
$$\overline{2\ 4\ 9\ 9\ 5}$$

Fred decided not to head south. (Smart kid!)

Instead, he started jogging west for a while before he headed back to KITTENS.

West

It was a beautiful Saturday morning. The sun was out. There was very little wind. Fred thought about Coalback's farm, his gym, and his electric heater store. *Somehow,* Fred thought, *they all felt dirty. Not just the dirt you can wash off with soap and water. It was a kind of heart dirty.**

Fred let go of those thoughts. He had pity for Coalback. He didn't hate him. Instead, as he jogged, he felt grateful for all the good things in his life.

After a couple of miles, Fred tried whistling. He had heard several students on campus whistling and it sounded like fun. This was the first time in his life that he tried. When he blew, nothing but air came out—no sound.

Then he tried yodeling. He had seen an old cowboy movie where the cowboy sat on his horse, played the guitar, and yodeled. Fred said, "Yo-del-lay-ee-who," but it didn't sound just right.

There are many things in life that take a lot of practice before they become easier. That's why we have A Row of Practice to help make addition and subtraction easier.

---

* Fred was searching for a word that not one person in a hundred ever uses in their vocabulary. Coalback is iniquitous. (eh-NICK-kwi-tis) To be iniquitous is to be dirty in your heart.

There were little signs beside the road.
They were as tall as Fred.

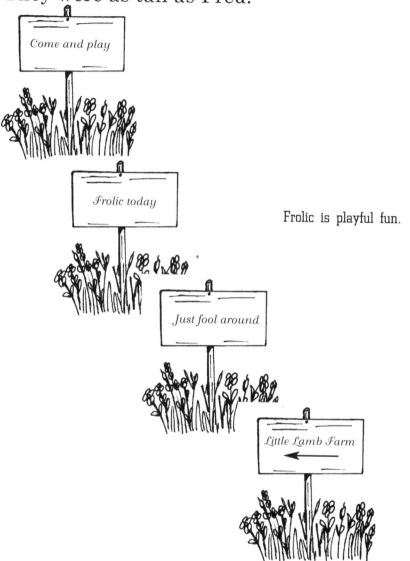

Come and play

Frolic today

Frolic is playful fun.

Just fool around

Little Lamb Farm

Fred followed the arrow.

He was expecting to see a lamb grazing in a
meadow. Isn't that how lambs frolic?

Not this lamb.

This lamb was sure to go, go, go.

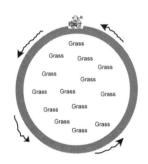

The lamb was racing along a gray concrete track around the circumference of the meadow.

Every time the lamb went around, Fred could hear him count: 235, 236, 237. . . .

Suddenly, it was quiet. The lamb had parked his car. He got out and wandered onto the grass to have a mid-morning snack.

Fred wanted to pet the lamb. He took off his shoes and socks. He liked the feel of grass on his bare feet.

He slowly walked over to the lamb. He didn't want to scare him. He wasn't sure what to do.

Fred smiled. *That will show the lamb that I'm friendly,* he thought.

Maybe I'll try some lamb talk. Fred said, "Baa."

The lamb stopped eating and looked up at him. Fred smiled again.

The lamb said, "Hey! That's my lunch and dinner that you are standing on in your bare feet. Can you imagine what you would feel like if I walked on your plate of food before you ate it?"

"Excuse me," Fred said. "I never thought of it that way." He quickly headed back to the circumference of the meadow.

As Fred was leaving, the lamb shouted, "And don't touch my car!"

Your Turn to Play

1. 235, 236, 237, 238, 239 . . . are consecutive natural numbers. We use consecutive natural numbers to count things. Name three consecutive natural numbers where the largest of them is 777.

2. When you are counting by twos, you use consecutive even numbers: 2, 4, 6, 8, 10, 12. . . .

Name three consecutive even numbers where the largest is 888.

3. The cardinality of {☎, ✈, ⌂} is 3. What is the cardinality of the empty set?

4. This is the set of natural numbers: {1, 2, 3, 4, . . . }. You use these numbers to count most things. Can you think of something you couldn't count with the natural numbers?

........**ANSWERS**.......

1. The three consecutive natural numbers where the largest of them is 777 are 775, 776, 777.

2. The three consecutive even numbers where the largest is 888 are 884, 886, and 888.

3. The cardinality of { } is 0.

4. The answer to the previous question was a BIG HINT. You can't use any of the natural numbers {1, 2, 3, 4, 5, 6, . . . } to name the number of members of the empty set.

You can't use the natural numbers to count the number of hippos that are sitting on your head.

You can't use the natural numbers to count the number of times your great-great-great-great grandmother used a computer.

You can't use the natural numbers to tell me how many natural numbers there are. (Translation: The cardinality of the set of natural numbers is not a natural number.)

A Row of Practice. *Do the whole row before you look at the answers.*

35	303	73	54	288
+ 89	− 6	+ 48	+ 67	+ 597
124	297	121	121	885

Chapter Twelve
Little Lamb Farm

F red stood on the gray concrete track. The lamb had left his car running. Presently,* the lamb finished his mid-morning snack and climbed back into his car.

"238, 239, 240 . . ." the lamb counted as he circled the meadow. Fred had stepped off the track so that he wouldn't be run over.

"Hi!" the runner said, as she headed up the path. "I see you have met my lamb."

Fred hoped that he hadn't done anything wrong. If this were like the Fun Farm that Coalback operated, Fred imagined that he would owe . . .

Admittance fee	$200.
Talking to lamb fee	30.
Standing on grass fee	7.
total	$237.

$$237 = 200 + 30 + 7$$
$$= 2 \text{ hundreds, } 3 \text{ tens, } 7 \text{ ones.}$$

---

* Presently = shortly, anon, in a moment.

Fred suddenly realized that you could break apart any number.

816 = 8 hundreds, 1 ten, 6 ones

5,304 = 5 thousands, 3 hundreds, 0 tens, 4 ones

7,926,841 = 7 millions, 9 hundred thousands, 2 ten thousands, 6 thousands, 8 hundreds, 4 tens, 1 one.

Fred had completely forgotten where he was. He got lost playing with the numbers.

"Hi!" she repeated. "Welcome to our farm."

"How much do I owe you?" Fred asked.

She smiled. "You don't owe anything. I'm glad to have you visit us. My name is Mary."

Finally, it all fit together for Fred: "little lamb," "was sure to go," "Mary."

Mary had a little lamb,
Its fleece was white as snow;
And everywhere that Mary went,
The lamb was sure to go.

Most kids learn this poem at home or at school. Fred had learned it when he read a biography of Thomas Edison. When Edison invented the phonograph in 1877, he recited this poem into his new machine. "Mary had a little lamb" was the second sound recording made in human history.

"Edison," Fred said. Again, he was lost in thought.

"No, my name is Mary," she answered. "Oh dear, it looks like my lamb has run over your shoes and socks." Fred had accidentally left them on the concrete track. She picked them up and handed them to Fred.

Fred put them on. He put on the socks before putting on the shoes. The commutative law does not hold for putting on shoes and socks. His socks had tire marks on them.

"Excuse me. Could I ask a rather personal question?" Fred began. "In the poem, your lamb is a little lamb, and you are a little girl going off to school. But you are older, and your lamb isn't little."

"Everyone asks that," she answered. "The poem was first published on May 24, 1830."

Fred broke apart the 24: 2 tens and 4 ones. He broke apart 1830: 1 thousand, 8 hundred, 3 tens and 0 ones.

Fred had another question: "Why does your lamb race around in a car? I thought the lamb was just supposed to follow you around."

"I'm a runner, and I had to buy a car for my lamb so that he could keep up with me."

241, 242, 243, 244. . . . The lamb kept zooming around the meadow.

"Doesn't he ever get tired of doing that— tired of going around in circles?" Fred asked. "I would think that would get boring after a while."

The lamb had overheard what Fred had asked Mary. He got out of his car and walked over to Fred.

"How can this be boring?" he began. "Every time I go around the circumference I get a new number. My next number is going to be 245. I never run out of new numbers. And every number is interesting."*

_____

* Many people don't know that *every* number is interesting. They know that 10 is interesting (the Ten Commandments). Twelve is a dozen eggs. Twenty is a score. 500 is the number of sheets in a ream of paper. They know that there are many numbers that are special in one way or another, but they don't know that every number has something interesting about it.

For my adult readers, here is the **proof** that every natural number is interesting. Suppose, for a moment, that there existed one or more uninteresting numbers. Consider the set of all those uninteresting numbers. We are assuming, for a moment, that this set is not the empty set { }.

Pick the smallest number in that set of uninteresting numbers. It might be 3,432,882,983,552,274, or it might be 435,662,007,298,981,112,083,452,477,290.

Think about that number for a moment. It is the smallest uninteresting number in the whole world. I could hang that number up on the wall, point to it, and say, "Look! This number is the smallest uninteresting number in the whole world."

But that would be a very interesting property.

But that would mean that there couldn't be a smallest uninteresting number.

But that would mean that there couldn't be a (non-empty) set of uninteresting numbers.

But that would mean that the set of uninteresting numbers is empty.

But that would mean that every number was interesting.

The lamb went back to his car and continued to drive around in circles.

Your Turn to Play

1. Break apart 3,982 into thousands, hundreds, etc.

2. This is the set of **natural numbers**: N = {1, 2, 3, 4, 5, 6, . . .}.

   This is the set of **whole numbers**: W = {0, 1, 2, 3, 4, 5, . . .}.

   The only difference between these two sets is that the set of whole numbers contains the number zero and the natural numbers doesn't.

   N ∪ W = ?

3. The whole numbers are much handier for counting the members in a set. (Translation: for finding the cardinality of a set.)

   There are lots of sets that I can describe that don't have any members. For example, the cardinality of the set of horses in your left ear is 0. The set of English words with a million letters has no members.

   Invent five more sets that have no members.

4. Fred weighs 37 pounds. The lamb weighs 50 pounds. Mary, 100. Draw a bar graph of their weights.

······· **ANSWERS** ·······

1. 3,982 = 3 thousands, 9 hundreds, 8 tens, 2 ones.

2. N ∪ W = {0, 1, 2, 3, . . . } which is W.

3. Actually, there is only one set that contains no members. It is the empty set. But it can be described in zillions of ways.

Here are my five descriptions. (Yours will probably be different. I would be *really* surprised if they were the same as mine!)

① The set of all 50-lb. apples.

② The set of all people that have 40 fathers.

③ The set of all glass pizzas.

④ The set of all 8-day weeks.

⑤ The set of all the children of Kingie.

4.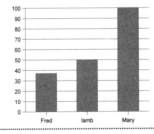

A Row of Practice. *Do the whole row before you look at the answers.*

47	805	56	74	632
+ 75	− 7	+ 94	+ 87	+ 599
122	798	150	161	1231

Chapter Thirteen
Secrets That Adults Know

Fred heard "245, 246," and then, suddenly, it was quiet. Then the lamb said, "Rats! Out of gas again."

He got out of his car and put a 5-gallon gas container in his teeth and trotted down the road. He was heading to the nearest gas station.

A gallon is equal to four quarts. So five gallons would be

$$
\begin{array}{r}
4 \\
4 \\
4 \\
4 \\
+\ 4 \\
\hline
\end{array}
$$

4 + 4 = 8
Then 8 + 4 = 12
Then 12 + 4 = 16
Then 16 + 4 = 20

20 quarts.

Time Out!

It's a secret, but many adults know that five 4s are equal to 20 without having to add them up.

They also know that eight 7s are equal to 56 . . . without having to add them up.

It is almost like magic. You say, "Eight 7s," and they say, "56."

You think $7 + 7 + 7 + 7 + 7 + 7 + 7 + 7$, and they think 8×7. (That's called, "Eight times seven.")

They just know that $8 \times 7 = 56$.

It's called **multiplication**. (mull-teh-pleh-KAY-shun) You know addition. They know multiplication.

In the next *Life of Fred* book, you can learn about the secrets of multiplication. Then when you buy eight 7-cent strawberries, you will know that they should cost 56¢.

Mary asked Fred, "Would you like to see the rest of the Little Lamb Farm?"

"Oh yes!" Fred said.

"I'll walk slowly, so you can keep up with me," she told him.

"That's okay," Fred said. "I've been jogging for many years. My lungs and heart are in much better condition than most other five-year-olds."

"Oh. I thought you were three or four years old," she said.

"I'm short for my age, but I really am five years old."

She started running. Fred couldn't keep up, so she slowed down. Mary was a runner. Fred was more of a jogger.

He could jog very long distances, but when you are only three feet tall, your legs are not very long.

 They ran down a path between the trees. There were five kids playing in the sunshine. "My other four are back at the house," she said.

Fred mentally added *Five plus four equals nine.* And then she added, "And our tenth is due in about six months." (Nine is a cardinal number. Tenth is an ordinal number.)

Fred slowed to a walk. Mary could see what was going through his mind and said, "Would you like to play with them?"

Fred thought,

Are milkshakes colder than light bulbs?

Does 2 + 2 equal 4?

Does the sun come up at dawn?

Is honey sweet?

and he said, "Yes. I think that would be fun."

Fred had not had much experience playing with other kids. This was going to be new for him. He wasn't sure what to expect.

He had read a lot of books and had learned a lot of things about math, science, history, poetry, geography, philosophy, Christianity, economics, linguistics (that's the study of languages), cooking, and knot tying. But he had never read much about kids playing without adult supervision.*

The five kids were playing tag. They were running around making lots of kid noises. Fred had never made a kid noise before. One girl yelled, "Yooowwweeeeooooiieeeaaa!" as she was being chased by another girl.

Fred tried running around in a circle, but he wasn't sure what to shout. Finally, he exclaimed, "Yell!" That didn't make much sense.

---

* Happily, he had not read *Lord of the Flies*, or he might have been scared silly.

A girl came up to Fred, tagged him, and said, "You're it." He didn't know what to do. He had not played tag before. He couldn't figure out why she said he was an "it." That was the wrong pronoun. She should have called him a "he," not an "it."

One of the boys explained to Fred, "Now you chase us and tag us." Fred ran and tagged one of the girls and said, "You're she."

Your Turn to Play

1. "Let's climb trees!" one of them yelled. They were tired of playing tag. Fred knew he would be looking at a **function**. The first set (called the **domain**) was the set of six kids {Anabel, Beatrice, Clarice, Don, Eddie, Fred}. The second set (the **codomain**) was the set of trees.

A function wasn't the two sets. A function is the rule which assigns to each member of the domain exactly one member of the codomain. (Translation: No kid climbs two trees. Every kid climbs a tree.)

Here was the function: Anabel → cherry tree
Beatrice → oak tree
Clarice → oak tree
Don → elm tree
Eddie → apricot tree
Fred → pine tree

Make up a function where the domain is {Ginny, Helen} and the codomain is {pie, cake, cookie}.

It's okay that Beatrice and Clarice both climbed the same tree. The rule is that each kid climbs exactly one tree—not that they all climb different trees.

·······ANSWERS·······

1. There are many possible answers.

You might have written: Ginny → pie

Helen → cake

or, maybe,   Ginny → cookie

Helen → cake

or, maybe,   Ginny → cake

Helen → cake.

Any of these would be fine.

Each member of the domain {Ginny, Helen} must have *exactly one* **image** in the codomain {pie, cake, cookie}.

This would not be a function: Ginny → pie
Helen → cake
Ginny → cookie

> *It's not a function because Ginny had two images.*

This would not be a function: Helen → pie

> *It's not a function because Ginny had no image.*

Functions are easy. You have to be able to count up to 1. Each member of the first set gets assigned ONE *member in the second set.*

Functions are tough. Chapter 11 in Life of Fred: Beginning Algebra is "Functions and Slope." Chapter 7 in Life of Fred: Advanced Algebra is "Functions." Chapter 2½ in Life of Fred: Trig is "Functions." Chapter 1 in Life of Fred: Calculus is "Functions." You will have plenty of time to learn how to count up to 1.

Chapter Fourteen
Down from the Trees

Fred was sitting up in his pine tree wondering what he was supposed to do next. "Everyone climb a tree" seemed like a silly game.

Then he heard, "CRACK!" He held on tightly. He hadn't fallen.

But Eddie had.

Everyone climbed down to look at Eddie. Eddie didn't look so good. He was holding his left arm. Anabel ran to the house to tell her dad. Eddie moaned a little.

Clarice asked him, "How is your arm?"

Eddie said, "My right arm is fine." He was trying to make a little joke. It wasn't very funny.

Roger (the dad) came running out of the house. Ginger, Harold, Iggy, and Johnny followed Roger. They had all been working in the kitchen and had flour all over themselves.

Clarice told her dad, "It's his left arm." Roger assigned each of his kids (the domain) something to do (the codomain):

Anabel → Go tell your mom.

Beatrice → Go with Anabel.

Clarice → Go get some blankets.

Don → Go with Clarice.

Eddie → Don't move.

Ginger → See if my cell phone is in the kitchen.

Harold → Check the bedroom for my cell phone.

Iggy → See if I've left my cell phone in the barn.

Johnny → Stay right here next to me. (Johnny is only two years old.)

Fred wasn't one of Roger and Mary's kids and didn't receive an assignment. Fred quietly prayed that Eddie would be okay.

Johnny was doing a good job of staying right next to his dad. His hair was almost white with flour.

Mary arrived, and Roger told her, "It's not serious—at most a broken arm."

Eddie stood up. Clarice and Don came back with a blanket. Mary carefully put it around Eddie's shoulders and said, "I guess we'd better get you off to the doc's to see if it's broken."

Clarice pointed to the tree that Eddie had been climbing and said, "That apricot tree has a broken arm." She was pointing to a *branch*. Some day Clarice would be a poet like Joyce Kilmer who wrote:

A tree that looks at God all day,

And lifts her leafy arms to pray;

A tree that may in Summer wear

A nest of robins in her hair. . . .

Some people think that trees don't have arms . . . or hair. Poets and artists can see what others don't see. That is what makes them special. They share what they see with the rest of us.

Ginger, Harold, and Iggy came running back. Ginger had found her dad's cell phone in the kitchen. It was covered with flour.

"No use us all going to the doc's," Mary said. "Who wants to stay here at the farm?"

The domain was all the people that Mary was talking to. The codomain was {Yes, No}.

Anabel → No   (She didn't want to stay at the farm.)
Beatrice → No   (She wanted to see what was going to happen.)
Clarice → No   (She was concerned about Eddie.)
Don → No   (He liked to go where Clarice went.)
Eddie → No   (He really had no choice!)
Ginger → No   (She always liked going on a trip.)
Harold → No   (He wondered how they would treat Eddie.)
Iggy → No   (He wasn't paying attention and just repeated
         what he heard everyone else say.)
Johnny → No   (He didn't want to be left alone at the farm.)
Roger → No   (He would help Mary with all the kids.)
Fred → No   (He didn't want to be left alone with that crazy lamb.)

This is a **constant function**. Every
member of the domain has the same image in
the codomain.

A function: No person gives two answers.

Every person gives an answer.

A constant function: Every person gives the same answer.

"Since everyone's going, I guess we'll need
to use the big car," Roger said.

Everyone climbed in.

As they drove off, Fred could see the lamb
putting gas in his little car. He heard
the little car being started. A moment
later he heard, " 247, 248. . . ."

As Roger drove out of the driveway,
he turned right and headed east. He was
driving back the way that
Fred had come. They passed
the front gate of the Fun
Farm.

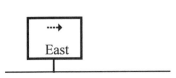

More letters had
fallen off.

Your Turn to Play

1. Is this a function?

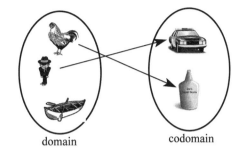

domain   codomain

2. Is this a function?

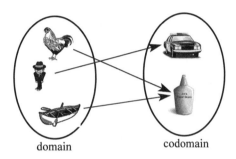

domain   codomain

3. Is this a function?

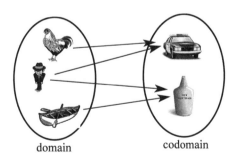

domain   codomain

......**ANSWERS**.......

The definition of a function is a rule that assigns to each member of the domain *exactly one* image in the codomain.

If you can count up to 1, you can check whether something is a function or not.

1. has one image.

    has one image.

    but doesn't have one image. (It has no image.)
       It's not a function.

2. has one image.

    has one image.

    has one image.
       It's a function.

3. has one image.

    has two images.

    has one image.
       It is not a function.

<u>A Row of Practice</u>. *Do the whole row before you look at the answers.*

67	402	94	55	363
+ 47	− 6	+ 48	+ 98	+ 788
114	396	142	153	1151

Chapter Fifteen
Meat Turnovers

Mary looked at her family in the big car. Her husband, Roger, and four of her kids—Ginger, Harold, Iggy, and Johnny—were a mess. They were covered with flour.

"What were you guys doing in the kitchen?" she asked them. "You were supposed to be making some meat turnovers for our lunch."

What a happy meat turnover should look like

Ginger said, "Daddy was cooking the meat on the stove. He asked us to make the dough for the turnovers."

Harold nodded and said, "That's right."

Iggy said, "Well. We got out the big bag of flour.* Harold and I carried it, because Johnny is only two, and he's too small."

Johnny said, "I watched."

Mary exclaimed, "But that doesn't explain how you all got covered with flour!"

Johnny said, "I didn't do it. I'm too small."

Mary asked Johnny, "Didn't do what?"

---

* With a family of eleven—2 adults + 9 kids—you do not buy the one-pound or the five-pound package of flour. That would be silly.

Johnny was quiet for a second and then said, "Ginger threw the first handful of flour."

Mary was quiet for another moment.

Johnny continued, "I only threw little handfuls, because I'm small."

Mary remained quiet. She was trying to imagine what the kitchen looked like.

Johnny added, "But Daddy was winning when Anabel came in to tell us about Eddie being hurt. Daddy's hands are big. They can hold a lot of flour. A flour fight is the funnest thing."

A Small Note

It will be a week or so before that mess is completely cleaned up. All the glasses and silverware had flour dust on them. There was flour in the toaster. Flour everywhere.

Seven plus eight make 15. Do you know what flour and water make? Flour + water = paste.

When Mary would pop Johnny into the bathtub later in the day, all the flour on his head would turn into sticky paste.

Harold reached into his pocket for a handkerchief. He needed to blow some paste out of his nose. He found that his pocket was filled with flour.

Don asked, "Does this mean we're not going to have turnovers for lunch?" In his heart, he really knew the answer to his question before he asked it. That kind of question is called a rhetorical question (re-TORE-ee-kel). That is a question to which no answer is expected. Don really wasn't asking a question. He was just complaining.

Roger turned the big car north. He was heading toward the hospital near KITTENS University.

KITTENS

north →

Fun
Farm

Little
Lamb   east →
Farm

They passed the giant green pickle head. This time it said:

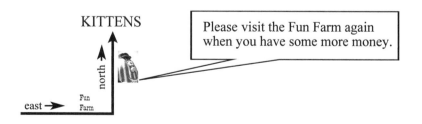

Johnny clapped his hands creating a little cloud of white flour. He liked the "pickle guy."

Eddie didn't clap his hands. Moving his left arm made it hurt more.

"Only three more minutes, and we will be there," Roger announced. With nine active kids and a wife who was frequently pregnant, Roger had driven this route to the hospital many times.

Beatrice said, "Daddy, let's play Questions." It was a game they often played in the car. Kids really like to play it.

Roger said, "Question number one. How many is one dozen?"

By the rules of the game, the youngest always gets first try to answer.

Johnny said, "I don't know. I pass it."

Then Iggy, who was second youngest, said, "Twelve."

Roger: "Question number two. What's the green stuff in plants called?"

Johnny passed on the question. So did Iggy, Harold, and Ginger. It was Fred's turn. He said, "Chlorophyll."

Roger: "Question number three. What is the third planet from the sun?"

Johnny: "Kansas."

Iggy passed on the question. Harold said, "The earth."

Roger: "Question number four. How many sides does a square have?"

Johnny giggled and said, "Two. The inside and the outside."

Your Turn to Play

1. What was the real answer to Roger's fourth question?

2. How many sides does a trapezoid have?

3. Which is longer, the diameter or the circumference of a circle?

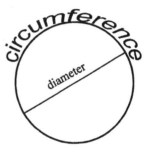

4. If a circle has a diameter of 5 inches, guess how long the circumference will be. (If you like, you can draw a circle with a diameter of 5 inches and try to measure the distance around the edge.)

. . . . **ANSWERS** . . . .

1. A square has four sides.

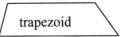

2. A trapezoid has four sides.

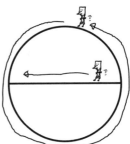

3. It takes a lot longer to walk all the way around a circle than to walk across it.

4. If the diameter of a circle is 5", then the circumference will be a little more than 15".

   Later, when you learn about decimals, you will be able to say that the circumference is *approximately*
   15.70796326794896619231321691398 inches.
It is *exactly* 5π.

Facts:
   π is pronounced PIE.
   π is written pi.
   π is a number.
   π is a little bigger than 3.
   π is also a letter in the Greek alphabet.

A Row of Practice.

53	207	64	374	753
+ 78	− 8	+ 84	− 27	+ 557
131	199	148	347	1310

Chapter Sixteen
The Game of Questions

Roger had gotten to, "Question number five: If you add together the number of plagues that Egypt had when Moses confronted Pharaoh to the number of days in a fortnight, what answer do you get?"*

Johnny said, "Three." Everyone laughed. Before Iggy started to answer, Johnny said, "But I'm right."

All the other people in the big car had something to say about Johnny's claim that his answer was correct.**

Anabel → "You're not right, Johnny."
Beatrice → "There are a lot more plagues than 3."
Clarice → "I think you were just guessing."
Don → "Three would be a good number of turnovers . . . for me."
Eddie → "Are we near the hospital?"
Ginger → "There are more than three days in a fortnight."
Harold → "You can't add, even if you knew there were 10 plagues."
Iggy → "And 14 days in a fortnight."
Roger → "It's okay, Johnny. Now let Iggy have a turn."
Mary → "Be nice. All of us make mistakes. Remember, Johnny is only two."

------

*   10 plagues
$\underline{+\ 14}$ days in a fortnight
        24

** If this looks to you like a function whose domain is all the other people in the car and whose codomain is their comments, you would be absolutely right.

Fred → "Johnny is right!"

Everyone looked at Fred. Some were wondering if he had sub-normal intelligence. They remembered that he was the one who said, "You're she," rather than "You're it" when playing tag.

Fred had taught for many years at KITTENS University. He had written many tests for his students. He had learned to *carefully* ask questions on the tests.

Anabel argued, "But Johnny didn't get the right answer. There are 10 plagues and 14 days in a fortnight."

Beatrice added, "And that makes 24."

Clarice replied, "And 24 is the right answer."

Fred smiled and said, "Yes, 24 is a right answer, but Johnny was also right when he said 'Three.'"

Don said, "You can't have two different answers that are both right."

Eddie yelled, "I see the hospital."

Roger pulled into a parking space, and everyone got out.

As they walked to the front door of the hospital, Mary asked Fred, "How could Johnny's answer be correct?"

Fred explained, "If your husband had asked what is the sum of the number of plagues and the number of days in a fortnight, then Johnny's answer would have been wrong."

Mary nodded in agreement.

"But," Fred continued, "Roger asked '. . . what answer do you get?' and Johnny got an answer of 'Three.' That is the correct answer to Roger's question."

Mary said, "Oh." She hadn't thought of that.

Roger walked up to the admitting nurse. Behind him were his nine kids, his wife, and Fred.

The nurse asked, "Which one is hurting today?" This wasn't the first time that this family had come to the hospital.* Once, they had even brought their lamb with them since the lamb would often follow Mary. (*"And everywhere that Mary went. . . ."*)

The nurse asked, "Was there an accident in the kitchen?" She was looking at all the flour on Roger's shirt.

---

* Or the second time. Or the third time. Or the fourth time. See how handy ordinal numbers can be!

"No. Eddie was playing outside," he said. "He fell out of a tree. His left arm."

"Well, come with me, young man, and we'll get you fixed up." Eddie and his mom followed the nurse.

Roger, his eight kids, and Fred stayed in the waiting room.

Don walked up to Roger and said, "Dad, I'm hungry." He had been thinking about those meat turnovers that they were going to have for lunch since he hadn't eaten much breakfast. He had been too busy playing with his brother Eddie at the breakfast table.

Don asked, "Is there a hospital cafeteria where I can get something to eat?" This was another of Don's rhetorical questions. They had all been to this hospital many times.

Ginger chimed in, "That would be fun."

Iggy said, "Me too." Iggy always liked to go along with whatever was happening. If Iggy had been a horse in a herd of horses, he would have had no trouble staying with the herd. If everyone was wearing a pink hat, Iggy would want one also.

If Iggy were full and everyone else was eating, Iggy would eat some more.

Roger said, "But this is the waiting room. Someone has to be here when Eddie is done."

"You stay here Dad," they all said. "We know the way to the cafeteria."

Roger nodded, and the kids headed down the hallway . . . everyone, except Fred. He was going to stay with Roger since he wasn't hungry.

Your Turn to Play

1. {Anabel, Don, Iggy} ∪ {Anabel, Don, Ginger}

2. You have learned all the addition facts. You know that $7 + 7 = 14$ and $9 + 9 = 18$. So now, you know all your two-times facts. You know that two times 7 equals 14. We write this as $2 \times 7 = 14$.

   Your question: $2 \times 9 = ?$

3. Just for fun. How much do eight 7-cent strawberries cost? (We did that three chapters ago.) It's okay if you don't remember what eight times seven equals. We will learn the multiplication facts later.

7 cents

4. Is this true: $2 \times 6 =$ one dozen?

5. $2 \times 100 = ?$

6. $2 \times 60 = ?$

. . . . . . .ANSWERS . . . .

1. {Anabel, Don, Iggy} ∪ {Anabel, Don, Ginger} =

   {Anabel, Don, Iggy, Ginger}.

(It's not correct to repeat yourself and write {Anabel, Anabel, Don, Don, Iggy, Ginger}. "No repetition" is a rule for writing sets using braces.)

2. 2×9 means

$$\begin{array}{r} 9 \\ +\ 9 \\ \hline 18 \end{array} \qquad 2 \times 9 = 18$$

3. 56¢. $8 \times 7 = 56$ It's also true that $7 \times 8 = 56$. (Multiplication is commutative.)

   There are only three or four multiplication facts that are hard to remember. Seven times eight equals fifty-six is one of them.

   Almost everyone knows their two-times tables. That is just doubling.

4. 2×6 means

$$\begin{array}{r} 6 \\ +\ 6 \\ \hline 12 \end{array}$$ and since 12 = one dozen, it is true that 2×6 = one dozen.

5. 2×100 means

$$\begin{array}{r} 100 \\ +\ 100 \\ \hline 200 \end{array} \qquad \text{so } 2 \times 100 = 200$$

6. 2×60 means

$$\begin{array}{r} 60 \\ +\ 60 \\ \hline 120 \end{array} \qquad \text{so } 2 \times 60 = 120$$

Chapter Seventeen
Bones

Roger was curious why Fred wasn't joining the other kids as they headed off to the cafeteria.

"Do you need some money?" he asked Fred.

"No," said Fred. He showed Roger the $100 that he had in his pocket. He offered Roger some of the Farmer's Nachos that were also in his pocket. Somehow the two nacho chips, with marshmallow sauce, and three jelly beans weren't very appealing to Roger.

There was a pause—a caesura.* Roger and Fred sat silently.

Fred wasn't thinking about food. He was thinking about something else, but was afraid to ask Roger directly.

He began indirectly and said, "Your oldest is Anabel?"

Roger nodded.

Fred asked, "And then Beatrice?"

---

* seh-ZOO-rah A caesura is a pause. From the Latin *caedere*, which means "to cut." You can have a caesura in music, when there is a break in a musical phrase, or in poetry in the middle of a line, or in conversation.

　　We also get the English word *concise* from the Latin *caedere*. Concise means to cut out all the extra words and get to the point.

Roger answered the question that a lot of people asked him, "Yes, we named our children alphabetically. First was **A**nabel, then **B**eatrice, then **C**larice, then **D**on, **E**ddie, **F**rankie, **G**inger, **H**arold, **I**ggy, and **J**ohnny."

"Frankie?" Fred asked. He knew that someone was missing between the **E** of Eddie and the **G** of Ginger.

Roger explained, "Frankie was born about six years ago, but lived only for a couple of days. Frankie is in Heaven right now and is very happy."

That was a mystery solved for Fred. He knew he wasn't the missing child in Roger and Mary's family even though his name began with **F**. Fred had known his real mom and dad. He remembered the day that they took him to King of French Fries where he was given Kingie.*

Mary joined them in the waiting room. "It's only a broken arm. They're setting Eddie's arm right now."

The Medical Details

There are two bones in your forearm—the radius and the ulna. It's easy to remember which is which: the <u>u</u>lna is <u>u</u>nderneath.

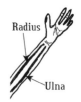

Radius

Ulna

---

* In *Life of Fred: Calculus*

Eddie had broken his ulna.

Breaking a bone is pretty common. Just falling down can sometimes break a bone in your hands, wrists, or feet.

To break the bigger bones (in the arms, legs, or hip) takes more force (falling out of a tree or an auto accident).

Setting a bone means to put it back into position so that it can heal. The two broken ends are aligned together.

Normal Conversation	Medical Language
forearm	radius or ulna
upper arm	humerus
ha-ha-ha	humorous
broken bone	fracture
setting the bone	reduction

After performing the reduction, they will put Eddie's arm in a plaster cast. That will hold the broken ends together until they heal.

"Where are the kids?" Mary asked. Roger pointed down the hall.

Mary asked Fred, "Didn't you want to go with them?"

Fred told her that he wasn't very hungry right now.

"Let's all go," Mary said. "The doc said that they gave Eddie a general anesthetic to set the bone, so it will be a while." (Translation: Often the doctors use a general anesthetic to cause the patient to sleep while they do the reduction so the patient doesn't feel any pain.)

"After he wakes up, they'll call us," Mary said.

Roger, Mary, and Fred headed down to the cafeteria to see how the eight were doing.

They headed east down the hall and then turned and headed south.

right angle

521 523 525 527 529 531 533 535 537 539

east ⋯➔

south ↓

Fred noticed that the room numbers on one side of the hall were consecutive odd numbers.

 Anabel had ordered an ice cream cone with a single scoop.

 Beatrice said, "Make mine a double."

"Double that!" said Clarice.

What his three sisters had started, was exactly what Don was going to continue. He got eight scoops. And Ginger got 16.

Your Turn to Play

1. And Harold got how many scoops?

2. And Iggy got how many?

3. And two-year-old Johnny got how many?

4. Fred, of course, didn't order any ice cream for himself. Instead, he looked at all those cones. The Anabel cone had one scoop. He wrote on a napkin $A_{nabel} = 1$, $B_{eatrice} = 2$, $C_{larice} = 4$, $D_{on} = 8$ and Fred began to play:

   If someone wanted 3, that would be A + B.

   If someone wanted 5, that would be A + C.

   If someone wanted 6, that's B + C.

   If someone wanted 7, that's A + B + C.

With 1, 2, 4, and 8, Fred found he could add up every number up to 15. For example, 13 would be 1 + 4 + 8.

If you include Ginger's 16 scoop, you can do every number up to what number?

. . . . **ANSWERS** . . . .

1. Harold ordered twice as many as Ginger's 16:   16

$$\begin{array}{r} 16 \\ +\ 16 \\ \hline 32 \end{array}$$

2. Iggy: 32

$$\begin{array}{r} 32 \\ +\ 32 \\ \hline 64 \end{array}$$

      64 scoops for Iggy

3. Johnny: 64

$$\begin{array}{r} 64 \\ +\ 64 \\ \hline 128 \end{array}$$

      128 scoops for Johnny.

4.

16 + 1	= 17
16 + 2	= 18
16 + 2 + 1	= 19
16 + 4	= 20
16 + 4 + 1	= 21
16 + 4 + 2	= 22
16 + 4 + 2 + 1	= 23
16 + 8	= 24
16 + 8 + 1	= 25
16 + 8 + 2	= 26
16 + 8 + 2 + 1	= 27
16 + 8 + 4	= 28
16 + 8 + 4 + 1	= 29
16 + 8 + 4 + 2	= 30
16 + 8 + 4 + 2 + 1	= 31

And just when we run out of numbers, Harold's 32 scoop cone will let us continue: $32 + 16 + 8 + 4 + 2 + 1 = 63$, then Iggy's 64 scoop will let us continue. It is no big surprise that $64 + 32 + 16 + 8 + 4 + 2 + 1$ will equal 127.

Chapter Eighteen
Eddie Ready

Roger was just in time to pay for all the ice cream that his kids had ordered. The sign on the wall read:

Roger began to add up

```
     1
     2
     4
     8
    16
    32
    64
+  128
```

> Ice Cream
> Cones
> only
> $1/scoop

Fred said, "$255."

He knew that the next cone would have cost $256 (128 + 128), so all the cones up to that would add to $255.

Roger didn't believe Fred. He added up the numbers. It came to $255.

Johnny's 128 scoops were starting to melt. The ice cream was running down his arm. Mary handed Johnny a napkin.

An announcement came over the hospital loudspeakers: Roger and Mary. Your son, Eddie, is done with his reduction. Please come and pick him up.

Roger, Mary, and Fred headed out the cafeteria door into the hallway. Then came Anabel, Beatrice, Clarice, Don, Ginger, Harold, and Iggy.

Iggy's 64-scoop cone barely made it through the doorway.

Johnny's 128 scoops didn't. The top 49 scoops were knocked off by the top of the doorway.

$$\begin{array}{r} 1\overset{1}{2}8 \\ -\ 49 \\ \hline \end{array}$$

79 scoops remained on his cone.

Forty-nine scoops landed on his head. When Mary would put Johnny in the bathtub later in the day, there would be both flour and ice cream to wash out of his hair.

When the eleven of them came into Eddie's room, he made a loud moan. Tears started to form in his eyes.

Mary came over and put her hand on his forehead.* "Oh, Eddie, my love. What hurts?" she asked him.

"I didn't get any ice cream!" he exclaimed.

Johnny ran up to Eddie and gave him a handful of his ice cream. Eddie = ☺.

Roger was so proud of his youngest son. Not too many two-year-olds would share their ice cream without being asked. He was going to pat Johnny on the head, but decided not to.

While Mary got Eddie ready to leave the hospital, Roger headed down to the business office to pay for Eddie. Fred joined him.

As they walked together, Roger took out his wallet and looked at how much money he had. He had six one-dollar bills, four five-dollar bills, and three ten-dollar bills.

"Our money system is crazy," Roger told Fred. "We have $1, $5, $10, $20, $50, and $100 bills." (THERE ARE $2 BILLS, BUT MANY PEOPLE DON'T KNOW ABOUT THEM.)

Fred nodded in agreement. He had thought about this before.

Roger continued, "We should have $1, $2, $4, $8, $16, $32, and $64 dollar bills. Then we

---

* If you want to become a news announcer on a national television show, you need to learn the most standard pronunciation of words. It's FOUR-id, not FOUR-head.

would only need to have one of each bill, and we could pay for anything."

(ANYONE WHO DID THE *Your Turn to Play* FOUR PAGES AGO KNOWS THIS.)

He explained to Fred that if he owed, say, $72, he would pay with one $64, one $8. Roger was delighted to explain some "heavy-duty"math to this little five-year-old. He didn't realize that Fred was a professor of math at KITTENS University.

Fred said, "Instead of ice-cream-scoop money ($1, $2, $4, $8, $16 . . .), all we need is:

$1, $3, $9, $27, $81. If everyone just carried one of each of these, you could buy anything up to $121.

"That's crazy," said Roger. "What if I wanted to buy something worth $5 from you?"

"Easy," said Fred. "You give me $9, and I'll give you $4 (= $1 + $3) in change."

Each Fred Buck is three times bigger than the previous one. The next one would be $81 + $81 + $81 = $243.

Your Turn to Play

The Fred Bucks come in these denominations (sizes):

$1, $3, $9, $27, $81. . . .

Suppose Roger had one of each Fred Buck.
Suppose Fred had one of each Fred Buck.

1. How would Roger pay Fred $26?
2. How would Roger pay Fred $7?
3. How would Roger pay Fred $13?
4. How would Roger pay Fred $14?
5. How would Roger pay Fred $22? (This one is hard.
It will probably take a couple of minutes to figure out.)

The advantage of Fred Bucks:

Your wallet or purse would never be overstuffed with bills. Carrying one of each denomination would be enough.

The disadvantage of Fred Bucks:

Unless you had Fred's math skills, you might go nuts trying to buy something for $61.

You give them $81.	$81 − $61 = $20	They now owe you $20.
They give you $27.	$27 − $20 = $7	You now owe them $7.
You give them $9.	$9 − $7 = $2	They now owe you $2.
They give you $3.	$3 − $2 = $1	You now owe them $1.
You give them $1.	$1 − $1 = $0	And the debt is paid.

. . . . ANSWERS . . . .

1. Roger owes Fred $26.
Roger pays Fred $27. $27 − $26 = $1.   Fred now owes Roger $1.

Fred pays Roger $1. $1 − $1 = $0.   The debt is paid.

2. Roger owes Fred $7.
Roger pays Fred $9. $9 − $7 = $2.   Fred now owes Roger $2.

Fred pays Roger $3. $3 − $2 = $1.   Roger now owes Fred $1.

Roger pays Fred $1. $1 − $1 = $0.   The debt is paid.

3. Roger owes Fred $13.
Roger pays Fred $9 + $3 + $1, and the debt is paid.

4. Roger owes Fred $14.
Roger pays Fred $27. $27 − $14 = $13.   Fred now owes Roger $13.

Fred pays Roger $9 + $3 + $1, and the debt is paid.

5. Roger owes Fred $22.
Roger pays Fred $27. $27 − $22 = $5.   Fred now owes Roger $5.

Fred pays Roger $9. $9 − $5 = $4.   Roger now owes Fred $4.

Roger pays Fred $3 + $1, and the debt is paid.

For Playing in the Car

If you took some 3×5 index cards and made them into ice-cream-scoop bills ($1, $2, $4, $8, $16 . . .) you could practice paying any amount that your parent challenged you to pay.

If you made Fred Bucks ($1, $3, $9, $27 . . .) you and someone else (parent, sister, brother) could play together.

Chapter Nineteen
Home

Roger, Mary, Anabel, Beatrice, Clarice, Don, Eddie, Ginger, Harold, Iggy, and Johnny climbed into their big car and drove off to the Little Lamb Farm.

Fred waved to them as they headed off. Eddie waved back with his right arm.

It was noon on Saturday. Fred had been to the Fun Farm on Snakefoot Road. He had seen Coalback and his sister arrested for some of the evil things they had done.

He had been to the Little Lamb Farm and had seen the lamb racing around the meadow. And Eddie with his fractured ulna.

Fred's socks had tire marks on them.

He reached into his pocket, and without thinking, took one of the Farmer's Nacho chips with marshmallow sauce and put it into his mouth. Yuck! It was stale. He spit it into a nearby garbage can. Fred had almost eaten something.

Fred walked back to the Math building. He climbed the two flights of stairs and walked down the hallway with the nine vending machines (four on one side and five on the other). He passed a cat with a big smile on its face.

He opened his office door.

Kingie was doing another oil painting.

Fred went to his desk and put the rest of the Farmer's Nachos in a drawer "for later." He handed Kingie the $100 that he had and told him that he would pay the rest back when he received his salary at the beginning of March.

Kingie had only one question: "Well, did you get a chance to pet a chicken?"

Fred lay down on his sleeping bag for a little noontime rest. He thought about Kingie's question and said, "No."

He was soon asleep.

In this book you completed the last addition fact: 9 + 7 = 16.

You now know all of them from 2 + 2 = 4 up to 9 + 9 = 18. The only thing left is practicing them in order to become a Wizard of Addition.

Here is a very special collection. <u>Five Rows of Practice</u>. They contain every single fact of addition.

84	256	66	373	525
+ 47	+ 362	+ 84	+ 527	+ 554
131	618	150	900	1079

84	557	67	373	925
+ 42	+ 364	+ 63	+ 459	+ 528
126	921	130	832	1453

84	532	69	488	279
+ 39	+ 362	+ 22	+ 268	+ 879
123	894	91	756	1158

58	166	77	242	655
+ 59	+ 698	+ 37	+ 479	+ 579
117	864	114	721	1234

59	418	34	222	2
+ 98	+ 346	+ 68	+ 758	+ 3
157	764	102	980	5

Index

After you have read the
*Life of Fred:
Elementary Series*
books, there are *Life of
Fred* books that will
take you all the way up
into your third year of
college.

Fred doesn't end.